SUPPLEMENT TO NORTH CAROLINA CRIMES

A GUIDEBOOK ON THE ELEMENTS OF CRIME

JESSICA SMITH　　　　　　　DECEMBER 2007

The School of Government at the University of North Carolina at Chapel Hill works to improve the lives of North Carolinians by engaging in practical scholarship that helps public officials and citizens understand and strengthen state and local government. Established in 1931 as the Institute of Government, the School provides educational, advisory, and research services for state and local governments. The School of Government is also home to a nationally ranked graduate program in public administration and specialized centers focused on information technology, environmental finance, and civic education for youth.

As the largest university-based local government training, advisory, and research organization in the United States, the School of Government offers up to 200 classes, seminars, schools, and specialized conferences for more than 12,000 public officials each year. In addition, faculty members annually publish approximately fifty books, periodicals, and other reference works related to state and local government. Each day that the General Assembly is in session, the School produces the *Daily Bulletin*, which reports on the day's activities for members of the legislature and others who need to follow the course of legislation.

The Master of Public Administration Program is a full-time, two-year program that serves up to sixty students annually. It consistently ranks among the best public administration graduate programs in the country, particularly in city management. With courses ranging from public policy analysis to ethics and management, the program educates leaders for local, state, and federal governments and nonprofit organizations.

Operating support for the School of Government's programs and activities comes from many sources, including state appropriations, local government membership dues, private contributions, publication sales, course fees, and service contracts. Visit www.sog.unc.edu or call 919.966.5381 for more information on the School's courses, publications, programs, and services.

Michael R. Smith, Dean
Thomas H. Thornburg, Senior Associate Dean
Frayda S. Bluestein, Associate Dean for Programs
Todd A. Nicolet, Associate Dean for Information Technology
Ann Cary Simpson, Associate Dean for Development and Communications
Bradley G. Volk, Associate Dean for Administration

FACULTY

Gregory S. Allison
Stephen Allred (on leave)
David N. Ammons
A. Fleming Bell, II
Maureen M. Berner
Mark F. Botts
Joan G. Brannon
Molly C. Broad
Michael Crowell
Shea Riggsbee Denning
James C. Drennan
Richard D. Ducker
Robert L. Farb
Joseph S. Ferrell
Milton S. Heath Jr.
Norma Houston (on leave)
Cheryl Daniels Howell
Joseph E. Hunt
Willow S. Jacobson
Robert P. Joyce
Diane M. Juffras
David M. Lawrence
Dona G. Lewandowski
James M. Markham
Janet Mason
Laurie L. Mesibov
Kara A. Millonzi
Jill D. Moore
Jonathan Q. Morgan
Ricardo S. Morse
David W. Owens
William C. Rivenbark
Dale J. Roenigk
John Rubin
John L. Saxon
Shannon H. Schelin
Jessica Smith
Karl W. Smith
Carl W. Stenberg III
John B. Stephens
Charles Szypszak
Vaughn Upshaw
A. John Vogt
Aimee N. Wall
Richard B. Whisnant
Gordon P. Whitaker
Eileen Youens

© 2008
School of Government
The University of North Carolina at Chapel Hill

Use of this publication for commercial purposes or without acknowledgment of its source is prohibited. Reproducing, distributing, or otherwise making available to a non-purchaser the entire publication, or a substantial portion of it, without express permission, is prohibited.

Printed in the United States of America

ISBN 978-1-56011-579-3

∞ This publication is printed on permanent, acid-free paper in compliance with the North Carolina General Statutes.

♳ Printed on recycled paper

TABLE OF CONTENTS

Chapter 3 **Participants in Crime** 1
    Principals—Acting in Concert / 1
    Aiding and Abetting / 1

Chapter 5 **General Crimes** 3
    Attempt / 3
    Conspiracy / 3

Chapter 6 **Homicide** 5
    First-Degree Murder / 5
    Second-Degree Murder / 6
    Voluntary Manslaughter / 6
    Involuntary Manslaughter / 6
    Death by Vehicle Offenses / 6
        I. Felony Death by Vehicle / 6
        III. Repeat Felony Death by Vehicle / 7

Chapter 7 **Assaults** 9
    Simple Assault / 9
    Assault Inflicting Serious Injury / 9
    Assault Inflicting Physical Injury by Strangulation / 9
    Assault with a Deadly Weapon / 10
    Assault with a Deadly Weapon with Intent to Kill / 10
    Discharging a Barreled Weapon or Firearm into Occupied Property / 11
    Assault on a Female / 11
    Simple Assault on a Handicapped Person / 11
    Aggravated Assault on a Handicapped Person / 11
    Assault on a Governmental Officer or Employee / 11
    Assault with a Firearm or Other Deadly Weapon on a Governmental Officer or Employee or Company or Campus Police Officer / 12

Chapter 8 **Threats, Harassment, Stalking, and Violation of Domestic Violence Protective Orders** 13
    Violation of a Domestic Violence Protective Order / 13

Chapter 9 **Abuse and Neglect** 15
    Child Abuse Inflicting Serious Physical Injury (Felony) / 15
    Contributing to a Juvenile's Being Delinquent, Undisciplined, Abused, or Neglected / 15
    Patient Abuse and Neglect / 16

Chapter 10 **Sexual Assaults** 17
    First-Degree Forcible Rape / 17
    First-Degree Forcible Sexual Offense / 18
    Sexual Activity by a Custodian / 18
    Indecent Liberties with a Child / 18
    Sexual Battery / 19

Table of Contents

Sex Offender Registration Offenses / 19
- I. Failure to Register, etc., as a Sex Offender / 19
- III. Knowingly Residing Near a School or Child Care Center / 20
- VI. Failing to Enroll in a Satellite-Based Monitoring Program / 20
- VII. Tampering with a Satellite-Based Monitoring Device / 20

Chapter 11 Crime against Nature, Incest, Indecent Exposure, and Related Offenses 21

Crime against Nature / 21

Chapter 12 Kidnapping and Related Offenses 23

First-Degree Kidnapping / 23

Chapter 13 Larceny, Possession of Stolen Goods, Embezzlement, and Related Offenses 25

Misdemeanor Larceny / 25
Felonious Larceny / 25
Possession of Stolen Goods—Misdemeanor / 25
Possession of Stolen Goods—Felony / 26
Receiving Stolen Goods—Misdemeanor / 26
Receiving Stolen Goods—Felony / 26
Larceny from a Merchant / 27
Organized Retail Theft / 27
- I. Conspiracy to Commit Retail Theft / 27
- II. Receiving or Possessing Retail Theft Property / 28

Financial Transaction Card Theft / 28
- I. Taking or Withholding a Card / 28

Embezzlement by Public Officers and Trustees / 29
Motor Vehicle Chop Shops / 29

Chapter 14 Robbery, Extortion, and Blackmail 31

Common Law Robbery / 31
Armed Robbery / 31

Chapter 15 Burglary, Breaking or Entering, and Related Offenses 33

First-Degree Burglary / 33

Chapter 16 Fraud, Forgery, False Pretenses, and Related Offenses 35

Obtaining Property by False Pretenses / 35
Residential Mortgage Fraud / 35
Food Stamp Fraud / 37
Fraudulently Obtaining Telephone Records / 37
False Statement to Procure Insurance Benefits / 37

Chapter 20 Bombing, Terrorism, and Related Offenses 39

Making a False Bomb Report / 39
- I. Making a False Bomb Report as to a Public Building / 39
- II. Making a False Bomb Report as to a Nonpublic Building or a Vehicle, Aircraft, Vessel, or Boat / 39

Making a False Report Concerning Mass Violence on Educational Property / 39

Chapter 21 Perjury, Bribery, and Other Crimes against the Administration of Justice 41

Common Law Obstruction of Justice / 41
Intimidating Witnesses / 41

	Perjury / 41
	Resisting, Delaying, or Obstructing an Officer / 42
	False Report to Law Enforcement Agencies or Officers / 42
	Interfering with an Emergency Communication / 42
Chapter 22	**Weapons Offenses 43**
	Possession of a Firearm by a Felon / 43
	Possession of Weapons on School Grounds / 43
	I. Possession of Firearms / 44
Chapter 24	**Obscenity and Related Offenses 45**
	Disseminating Obscenity / 45
	Third-Degree Sexual Exploitation of a Minor / 45
Chapter 25	**Gambling, Bingo, and Raffles 47**
	Gambling / 47
Chapter 27	**Drug Offenses 49**
	Sale or Delivery of a Controlled Substance / 49
	Manufacture of a Controlled Substance / 49
	Possession of a Controlled Substance / 49
	Possession of a Controlled Substance with Intent to Manufacture, Sell, or Deliver / 50
	Manufacture, Sale, Delivery, or Possession of a Controlled Substance with Intent to Manufacture, Sell, or Deliver at or Near A School, Child Care Center, or Public Park / 50
	Trafficking / 51
	I. Trafficking in Marijuana / 51
	Maintaining a Store, Dwelling, Vehicle, Boat, or Other Place for Use, Storage, or Sale of Controlled Substances / 51
	Inhaling Toxic Fumes / 52
	Possession of a Toxic Substance / 52
	Sale, etc., of a Toxic Substance / 52
	Manufacture, etc., of an Alcohol Vaporizing Device / 52
Chapter 28	**Motor Vehicle Offenses 53**
	Driving While License Revoked or Disqualified / 53
	I. Driving While License Revoked / 53
	Impaired Driving and Related Offenses / 53
	I. Impaired Driving / 53
	V. Habitual Impaired Driving / 54
	VI. Driving by a Person under 21 Years of Age after Consuming Alcohol or Drugs / 54
	Serious Injury by a Vehicle / 54
	I. Felony Serious Injury by a Vehicle / 54
	School Bus Offenses / 54
	III. Felony Passing or Failure to Stop for a School Bus / 54
	IV. Use of a Cell Phone When Driving a School Bus / 55
	Failure to Stop, Move Over, or Slow Down for an Emergency Vehicle / 55
	III. Failure to Move Over or Slow Down for a Stopped Emergency or Public Service Vehicle / 55

INTRODUCTION

This book supplements *North Carolina Crimes: A Guidebook on the Elements of Crime* (UNC School of Government, 6th ed. 2007). It includes cases decided and legislation enacted through December 31, 2007. Chapter and page numbers used throughout this supplement refer to chapters and pages in the main edition.

CHAPTER 3
PARTICIPANTS IN CRIME (PAGE 17)

PRINCIPALS—ACTING IN CONCERT (PAGE 21)

Notes (page 21)

Element (1) (page 21). A defendant who participated in two crimes with an accomplice, remained in a truck during a third crime—a store robbery—and then drove away with the accomplice was constructively present during the store robbery (___ N.C. App. ___, 642 S.E.2d 491).

Element (2) (page 21). A homicide conviction on the theory of acting in concert was proper where the defendant and another person shared a common purpose of forcibly confronting the victim with a weapon (___ N.C. App. ___, 638 S.E.2d 36). For other cases in which the evidence was sufficient to establish a common purpose, see ___ N.C. App. ___, 653 S.E.2d 6 (the defendant, a county jail shift supervisor, shared a common purpose with another during a beating of a prisoner); 181 N.C. App. 209 (common purpose to commit larceny); ___ N.C. App. ___, 641 S.E.2d 380 (armed robbery); ___ N.C. App. ___, 644 S.E.2d 615 (armed robbery).

AIDING AND ABETTING (PAGE 22)

Notes (page 23)

Generally (page 23). For a case in which the defendant's money laundering activity constituted sufficient evidence to support a conviction of aiding and abetting obtaining property by false pretenses, see ___ N.C. App. ___, 651 S.E.2d 598.

Charging issues (page 24). The trial judge could instruct the jury on aiding and abetting even though the indictment alleged acting in concert (___ N.C. App. ___, 651 S.E.2d 598).

CHAPTER 5
GENERAL CRIMES (PAGE 47)

ATTEMPT (PAGE 49)

Notes (page 50)

Element (1) (page 50). For a case in which the evidence was sufficient to establish intent to commit robbery, see ___ N.C. App. ___, 645 S.E.2d 835). In a sexual assault case, the evidence was sufficient to establish that the defendant intended to engage in vaginal intercourse with the victim; the defendant repeatedly asked the victim to have intercourse with him, told her that he wanted to be "inside [her]" and be "[her] first," and performed other kinds of sexual acts on her (___ N.C. App. ___, 647 S.E.2d 440). The evidence was sufficient to establish an intent to commit rape when the defendant, whose pants were unzipped, straddled the victim and tried to pull up her shirt (___ N.C. App. ___, 653 S.E.2d 249).

Element (2) (page 50). For a case in which there was sufficient evidence of an overt act in an attempted robbery case, see ___ N.C. App. ___, 645 S.E.2d 835. The evidence of an overt act was sufficient in an attempted first-degree sexual offense case where there was no violence but the evidence showed that the defendant removed his pants, walked into the room where the seven- or eight-year-old victim was seated, stood in front of her, and asked her to put his penis in her mouth (___ N.C. App. ___, 642 S.E.2d 509).

Attempted assault (new note). Attempted assault is not a crime; because an assault includes an overt act or attempt, or the unequivocal appearance of an attempt, an attempted assault would be an attempt to attempt (181 N.C. App. 302).

CONSPIRACY (PAGE 52)

Notes (page 53)

Element (1) (page 53). Other cases in which there was sufficient evidence of an agreement include 181 N.C. App. 196 (conspiracy to commit first-degree murder) and ___ N.C. App. ___, 648 S.E.2d 865 (conspiracy to traffic in cocaine by possession).
    For a case in which the evidence was insufficient to establish an express or implied agreement to traffic in cocaine by transportation, see ___ N.C. App.

___, 641 S.E.2d 858 (the defendant was stopped while driving a vehicle with one passenger, cocaine was found in the trunk of the vehicle, both men were nervous, and the vehicle had an odor of air freshener; there was no evidence of conversation between the driver and the passenger, unusual movements or actions, large amounts of cash, possession of weapons, or anything else suggesting an agreement).

CHAPTER 6
HOMICIDE (PAGE 63)

FIRST-DEGREE MURDER (PAGE 65)

Statute **(page 65).** In 2007 the General Assembly amended the murder statute, G.S. 14-17, to provide that a defendant convicted of first-degree murder who was under age 18 at the time of the murder may not be sentenced to death (S.L. 2007-81). Such a defendant will be sentenced to life imprisonment without parole (S.L. 2007-81). This change became effective June 14, 2007.

Notes **(page 66)**

Element (3)(a)(ii) (page 67). For cases in which there was sufficient evidence of a specific intent to kill, see 174 N.C. App. 745 (the evidence showed that, in order to avoid paying child support, the defendant abandoned an infant in 30-degree weather and in a remote, dilapidated shed where she would not likely be found), and ___ N.C. App. ___, 653 S.E.2d 174 (the evidence showed that the defendant had a history of beating the victim, hit the victim without provocation on the day of the killing, told others to tell him good-bye, and told the victim to say his prayers; the cause of death was strangulation and blunt trauma; and the defendant attempted to conceal the body and evidence).

For cases in which the evidence sufficiently established premeditation and deliberation, see 168 N.C. App. 614 (the defendant attacked an unsuspecting victim and then made statements indicating that he intended to kill the victim) and 171 N.C. App. 504 (the wounds inflicted by the defendant were brutal, the blows were multiple, the victim had harassed the defendant, and the defendant left the scene of the crime).

Element (3)(c) (page 68). For a more lengthy discussion of the continuous transaction doctrine and the merger rule, see Robert L. Farb, *North Carolina Capital Case Law Handbook*, pp. 17–18 and 149–52 (UNC School of Government, 2d ed. 2004) [hereinafter *Capital Handbook*].

For an additional case supporting the statement in the last paragraph of this note that for felony-murder to apply, the defendant, co-conspirators, aiders or others acting in concert with the defendant must have committed the homicide, see ___ N.C. App. ___, 648 S.E.2d 896.

Lesser-included offenses (page 70). For a more detailed discussion of the lesser-included offenses of first-degree murder, see *Capital Handbook* at pp. 139–43.

SECOND-DEGREE MURDER (PAGE 70)

Notes (page 71)

Element (3) (page 71). There was sufficient evidence of malice when the defendant drove knowing that his license had been revoked, took the vehicle without permission, and fled from the police (____ N.C. App. ___, 652 S.E.2d 299).

VOLUNTARY MANSLAUGHTER (PAGE 72)

Notes (page 72)

Attempted voluntary manslaughter (page 73). The following should be added at the end of the second paragraph of this note: Jury verdicts of guilty of assault with a deadly weapon inflicting serious injury and attempted voluntary manslaughter concerning the same victim are mutually exclusive when the jury rejected a felonious assault charge involving an intent to kill (174 N.C. App. 755).

Multiple convictions (new note). Attempted voluntary manslaughter is a lesser-included offense of a felonious assault offense that includes an element of intent to kill and the defendant may not be convicted of both (174 N.C. App. 755).

INVOLUNTARY MANSLAUGHTER (PAGE 74)

Notes (page 74)

Element (3)(b) (page 75). For an additional case upholding a conviction based on a mishap with a firearm, see ___ N.C. App. ___, 640 S.E.2d 757.

DEATH BY VEHICLE OFFENSES (PAGE 76)

Statute (page 76). Effective August 30, 2007, the General Assembly amended G.S. 20-141.4(a6), as discussed below under "III. Repeat Felony Death by Vehicle" (S.L. 2007-493, sec. 15). To save space, the revised statute is not reproduced here.

I. Felony Death by Vehicle (page 77)

Notes (page 77)

License revocation (new note). Conviction of any offense under G.S. 20-141.4 results in a license revocation [G.S. 20-17(a)(9); S.L. 2007-493, sec. 2].

III. Repeat Felony Death by Vehicle (page 78)

Legislation enacted in 2007 amended G.S. 14-141.4(a6) as follows: (1) adding the requirement that pleading and proof of previous convictions must be in accordance with G.S. 15A-928, and (2) deleting the clause stating that the basis of a previous conviction under G.S. 14-17 or G.S. 14-18 is determined from the face of the indictment.

CHAPTER 7
ASSAULTS (PAGE 81)

SIMPLE ASSAULT (PAGE 84)

Notes (page 84)

Attempted assault (new note). Attempted assault is not a crime; because an assault includes an overt act or attempt, or the unequivocal appearance of an attempt, an attempted assault would be an attempt to attempt (181 N.C. App. 302).

ASSAULT INFLICTING SERIOUS INJURY (PAGE 86)

Notes (page 86)

Element (2) (page 86). Add the following at the end of the first paragraph: However, if reasonable minds could differ as to whether the injury was serious, it is error for the trial court to give such a peremptory instruction (___ N.C. App. ___, 644 S.E.2d 615) (error to give peremptory instruction as to gunshot wound to a leg).

Add the following to the end of the second paragraph of this note: There was sufficient evidence of serious injury when a bullet went completely through the victim's leg and the victim was unable to drive himself to the hospital, was treated at the hospital for the wound, and suffered pain for two or three weeks (___ N.C. App. ___, 644 S.E.2d 615).

ASSAULT INFLICTING PHYSICAL INJURY BY STRANGULATION (PAGE 88)

Notes (page 88)

Element (3) (page 88). The *North Carolina Criminal Pattern Jury Instructions* define "strangulation" as "a form of asphyxia characterized by closure of the blood vessels and/or air passages of the neck as a result of external pressure on the neck brought about by hanging, ligature, or the manual assertion of pressure" (N.C.P.I.—Crim. 208.61, n.1).

The evidence was sufficient when it showed that the defendant grabbed the victim by the throat causing her to have difficulty breathing; the State is not required to prove that the victim had a complete inability to breathe (___ N.C. App. ___, 643 S.E.2d 637).

Lesser-included offenses (new note). Assault on a female is not a lesser-included offense of assault inflicting physical injury by strangulation [State v. Brunson, ___ N.C. App. ___, ___ S.E.2d ___ (Dec. 4, 2007)].

ASSAULT WITH A DEADLY WEAPON (PAGE 88)

Notes (page 89)

Element (2) (page 89). The following should be added at the end of the first paragraph: The trial court did not err when it instructed the jury that a knife is a deadly weapon, where the evidence showed that the victim suffered life threatening injuries but the knife was not introduced or described in detail at trial (___ N.C. App. ___, 650 S.E.2d 639). When there is a factual issue concerning whether or not a weapon is a deadly weapon, the judge errs by failing to instruct on a lesser-included nondeadly weapon assault offense (___ N.C. App. ___, 651 S.E.2d 291).

The following should be added to the third paragraph of this note: The Court of Appeals has held that a defendant's use of his hands in conjunction with water constituted a deadly weapon (___ N.C. App. ___, 650 S.E.2d 29). In that case, the defendant pushed the victim into a river, forcibly held his head underwater, and pushed the victim back underwater after the victim managed to get a breath. The court emphasized that because the defendant did not use his hands alone, the State was not required to present evidence as to the size or condition of the victim and the defendant.

The following should be added at the end of this note: Assault with a firearm can be accomplished when the defendant reaches for but does not succeed in touching the weapon (181 N.C. App. 302).

ASSAULT WITH A DEADLY WEAPON WITH INTENT TO KILL (PAGE 91)

Notes (page 91)

Element (3) (page 91). Even though the defense offered unrebutted expert testimony that the defendant could not form an intent to kill due to mental disorders and an excessive dose of medication, there was sufficient evidence as to that element given the number of stab wounds the defendant inflicted on the victims and the manner in which the stabbings took place (the defendant stabbed one victim 22 times, knocked her to the ground, got on top of her, and continued stabbing her, and he stabbed another victim five times, inflicting serious injuries) as well as the defendant's statement that he attacked one of the victims (183 N.C. App. 93).

DISCHARGING A BARRELED WEAPON OR FIREARM INTO OCCUPIED PROPERTY (PAGE 95)

Notes **(page 95)**

Element (3) (page 95). For another case in which there was sufficient evidence that the defendant had reasonable grounds to believe that a building was occupied, see ___ N.C. ___, 652 S.E.2d 241.

ASSAULT ON A FEMALE (PAGE 98)

Notes **(page 98)**

Element (3) (new note). The age requirement for this offense pertains only to the defendant; there is no age requirement for the victim (___ N.C. App. ___, 647 S.E.2d 440).

SIMPLE ASSAULT ON A HANDICAPPED PERSON (PAGE 101)

Related Offenses Not in This Chapter **(page 101).** Add the following offense to this section:
Injuring or killing law-enforcement agency animal or assistance animal (G.S. 14-163.1)

AGGRAVATED ASSAULT ON A HANDICAPPED PERSON (PAGE 102)

Related Offenses Not in This Chapter **(page 102).** This section should state:
See the offenses listed under "Simple Assault on a Handicapped Person."

ASSAULT ON A GOVERNMENTAL OFFICER OR EMPLOYEE (PAGE 102)

Notes **(page 103)**

Charging both assault on a governmental officer or employee and resisting arrest (page 104). For an additional case supporting the statement in this note that convictions for both offenses are proper when based on different conduct, see ___ N.C. App. ___, 651 S.E.2d 584.

ASSAULT WITH A FIREARM OR OTHER DEADLY WEAPON ON A GOVERNMENTAL OFFICER OR EMPLOYEE OR COMPANY OR CAMPUS POLICE OFFICER (PAGE 105)

Notes (page 105)

Element (1) (page 105). The following should be added to this note: An assault with a firearm was accomplished when the defendant reached for, but did not succeed in touching, a weapon (181 N.C. App. 302).

Element (2) (page 107). When there is a factual issue as to whether a deadly weapon was used, a trial court must submit to the jury the lesser-included offense of assault on a governmental officer or employee (___ N.C. App. ___, 650 S.E.2d 29).

CHAPTER 8
THREATS, HARASSMENT, STALKING, AND VIOLATION OF DOMESTIC VIOLENCE PROTECTIVE ORDERS (PAGE 127)

VIOLATION OF A DOMESTIC VIOLENCE PROTECTIVE ORDER (PAGE 138)

Statute **(page 138).** Effective December 1, 2007, G.S. 50B-4.1 was amended (S.L. 2007-190) by adding a new subsection (g) as follows:

> (g) Unless covered under some other provision of law providing greater punishment, any person who, while in possession of a deadly weapon on or about his or her person or within close proximity to his or her person, knowingly violates a valid protective order as provided in subsection (a) of this section by failing to stay away from a place, or a person, as so directed under the terms of the order, shall be guilty of a Class H felony.

Punishment **(page 139).** Pursuant to new subsection (g), reproduced above, any person who, while in possession of a deadly weapon, knowingly violates a valid protective order by failing to stay away from a place, or a person, as directed under the terms of the order, is guilty of a Class H felony. The additional facts must be pleaded and proved beyond a reasonable doubt at trial.

This note discusses the fact that a person who commits a felony knowing that the behavior is prohibited by a valid domestic violence protective order is guilty of an offense one class higher than the felony committed. A temporary restraining order granted in a Chapter 50 civil action (divorce from bed and board) was issued pursuant to Chapter 50B and thus qualifies as a protective order for purposes of the enhanced punishment (___ N.C. App. ___, 649 S.E.2d 444, *review allowed*, N.C. Nov. 8, 2007).

CHAPTER 9
ABUSE AND NEGLECT (PAGE 141)

CHILD ABUSE INFLICTING SERIOUS PHYSICAL INJURY (FELONY) (PAGE 145)

Notes (page 145)

Elements (2)(a) and (2)(b) (page 145). An additional case supporting the statement in this note that the State must prove only that the defendant intentionally inflicted injury that was serious and need not prove that the defendant intended to inflict serious injury is ___ N.C. App. ___, 646 S.E.2d 613.

The evidence was sufficient to show that the defendant acted intentionally when he beat the victim with a belt for 40 to 100 minutes; the victim bled, was short of breath due to asthma, and vomited; the victim's arms were almost entirely covered in bruises, his legs were swollen and puffy, and his buttocks were black and blue; the victim was hospitalized after the incident and was in pain for two weeks; and a medical expert testified that the victim's injuries were moderately to seriously severe, could have resulted in complications, and were nonaccidental. (___ N.C. App. ___, 646 S.E.2d 613).

Element (3). (page 145). The evidence was sufficient to establish serious physical injury when the defendant beat the victim with a belt for 40 to 100 minutes; the victim bled, was short of breath due to asthma, and vomited; the victim's arms were almost entirely covered in bruises, his legs were swollen and puffy, and his buttocks were black and blue; the victim was hospitalized after the incident and was in pain for two weeks; and a medical expert testified that the victim's injuries were moderately to seriously severe and could have resulted in complications (___ N.C. App. ___, 646 S.E.2d 613).

CONTRIBUTING TO A JUVENILE'S BEING DELINQUENT, UNDISCIPLINED, ABUSED, OR NEGLECTED (PAGE 148)

Related Offenses Not in This Chapter (page 150). The following should be added to this note:
Selling alcohol to underage person [G.S. 18B-302(a)]
Giving alcohol to underage person [G.S. 18B-302(a1)]

PATIENT ABUSE AND NEGLECT (PAGE 150)

Punishment (page 150). Effective December 1, 2007, the General Assembly amended G.S. 14-32.2(b) to increase, from a Class A1 misdemeanor to a Class H felony, the punishment for this offense when elements (1) through (4) and (5)(d) exist (S.L. 2007-188).

CHAPTER 10
SEXUAL ASSAULTS (PAGE 155)

FIRST-DEGREE FORCIBLE RAPE (PAGE 157)

Notes (page 158)

Element (1) (page 158). The victim's testimony that the defendant "had sex" with her along with other evidence was sufficient to establish penetration (___ N.C. App. ___, 645 S.E.2d 166).

Element (3) (page 158). A conviction was proper where constructive force could be inferred from the parent–child relationship between the defendant and the victim (___ N.C. App. ___, 647 S.E.2d 440).

Element (5)(a) (page 159). A defendant's hands are not dangerous or deadly weapons for purposes of first-degree rape or first-degree sexual offense; the statutes require that an "external" weapon be used [State v. Adams, ___ N.C. App. ___, ___ S.E.2d ___ (Dec. 18, 2007)].

When the State alleges that use or display of a dangerous or deadly weapon elevates a rape or sexual offense to first-degree and the jury is not instructed on the theory of acting in concert or aiding and abetting, the evidence must support a finding that the defendant personally used or displayed the weapon [State v. Person, ___ N.C. App. ___, ___ S.E.2d ___ (Dec. 18, 2007)].

Attempt (page 160). For a case in which the evidence was not sufficiently conflicting on penetration as to require an instruction on attempted rape, see ___ N.C. App. ___, 651 S.E.2d 924).

Lesser-included offenses (page 160). Sexual battery is not a lesser-included offense of first-degree or second-degree rape [State v. Kelso, ___ N.C. App. ___, ___ S.E.2d ___ (Dec. 18, 2007); ___ N.C. App. ___, 651 S.E.2d 231].

Multiple prosecutions (page 161). A defendant may not be convicted for both forcible rape and statutory rape based on the same act; the same rule applies to sexual offenses (___ N.C. App. ___, 648 S.E.2d 886).

FIRST-DEGREE FORCIBLE SEXUAL OFFENSE (PAGE 167)

Notes (page 168)

Attempt (page 169). For a case in which the evidence on penetration was not conflicting and did not require an instruction on attempted anal intercourse, see State v. Person, ___ N.C. App. ___, ___ S.E.2d ___ (Dec. 18, 2007).

Punishment for separate acts (page 169). This note includes a "but see" cite to 132 N.C. App. 453, as a case holding that when both cunnilingus and inserting an object into a minor's genital area occurred during a single transaction, only one conviction was allowed. The North Carolina Court of Appeals has since noted that the cited case dealt with the separate issue of unanimity of the jury verdict (___ N.C. App. ___, 651 S.E.2d 279 at n.5). That case also stated in dicta that a defendant may be punished for separate and distinct sexual acts that occurred in a single transaction [___ N.C. App. ___, 651 S.E.2d 279 at n.7 (stating that even if the defendant had preserved his challenge to convictions for both cunnilingus and fellatio that occurred in the same transaction, it would fail]. That dicta in turn cited a recent indecent liberties case, which held that the defendant's action of engaging in three distinct sexual acts on the victim in one transaction—fondling her breasts, performing oral sex on her, and having sexual intercourse with her—supported three separate indecent liberties convictions [___ N.C. App. ___, 643 S.E.2d 34 (distinguishing 178 N.C. App. 337 by stating that in that case the defendant's actions all involved the same sexual contact—touching—whereas this case involved three distinct sexual acts)].

SEXUAL ACTIVITY BY A CUSTODIAN (PAGE 176)

Notes (page 176)

Element (1) (page 176). An independent contractor who provides medical care to prisoners in a county jail can be convicted of this offense (___ N.C. App. ___, 643 S.E.2d 620, review allowed, N.C. Aug. 28, 2007).

INDECENT LIBERTIES WITH A CHILD (PAGE 180)

Notes (page 180)

General discussion of Elements (2)(a) and (2)(b) (page 180). The defendant's act of masturbating while lying in a bed with the victim and watching a pornographic movie constituted an indecent liberty even though the defendant did not touch the victim (___ N.C. App. ___, 642 S.E.2d 454).

The defendant's act of "french kissing" the victim constituted a lewd or lascivious act (___ N.C. App. ___, 642 S.E.2d 454).

There was insufficient evidence to support an indecent liberties conviction when the victim, who testified to many acts performed by the defendant, provided no testimony in support of this charge; the only evidence supporting the charge was a doctor's testimony that the victim "described that [the defendant] wanted her to perform fellatio, or put his penis in her mouth, but that she didn't want to do that"; the doctor's testimony raised only a suspicion or conjecture (___ N.C. App. ___, 647 S.E.2d 440).

Element (2)(a)(i) (page 181). For another case in which there was sufficient evidence that the defendant assaulted the victim for the purpose of sexual desire, see ___ N.C. App. ___, 648 S.E.2d 886).

Multiple prosecutions (page 182). The defendant's acts of engaging in three distinct sexual acts on the victim in one transaction—fondling her breasts, performing oral sex on her, and having sexual intercourse with her—supported three separate indecent liberties convictions (___ N.C. App. ___, 643 S.E.2d 34). The court distinguished 178 N.C. App. 337, discussed in the text, stating that in that case the defendant's actions all involved the same sexual contact—touching—whereas the case before it involved three distinct sexual acts (___ N.C. App. ___, 643 S.E.2d 34).

SEXUAL BATTERY (PAGE 187)

Notes **(page 188)**

Relationship to rape (new note). Sexual battery is not a lesser-included offense of second-degree rape (___ N.C. App. ___, 651 S.E.2d 231).

SEX OFFENDER REGISTRATION OFFENSES (PAGE 189)

Statute **(page 189).** Legislation enacted in 2007 amended a number of the provisions related to the registration offenses and enacted several new provisions (S.L. 2007-213). These amendments are discussed in detail in Chapter 7, "Criminal Law and Procedure," in *North Carolina Legislation* 2007 (UNC School of Government, 2007), available online at www.sog.unc.edu/pubs/nclegis/nclegis2007/index.html. This supplement discusses only the significant changes affecting the elements of the sex offender registration crimes.

I. Failure to Register, etc., as a Sex Offender (page 198)

Notes **(page 198)**

Elements (3)(b) and (3)(g). Legislation enacted in 2007 (S.L. 2007-213, sec. 9A) modified the registration requirements for a change of address in G.S. 14-208.9(a). The statute has required the person to report a change of address to the sheriff of the county where the person was last registered. The amendments add the requirement that when a person moves to another county, he or she also must report in person to the sheriff of the *new county* and provide written notice of the person's address not later than 10 days after the move.

III. Knowingly Residing Near a School or Child Care Center (page 201)

Notes (page 201)

Changes in ownership after residency is established (page 201). Due to 2007 legislative changes (S.L. 2007-213, sec. 10), the last sentence of this note should now read as follows: Residency is established when a person purchases or leases the residence or lives with a child or sibling 18 or older or with a parent, grandparent, legal guardian, or spouse who has established residence [G.S. 14-208.16(d)].

VI. Failing to Enroll in a Satellite-Based Monitoring Program (page 203)

Related Offenses Not in This Chapter (page 203). Failing to provide information to or cooperate with the Department [G.S. 14-208.44(c)]

VII. Tampering with a Satellite-Based Monitoring Device (page 203)

Elements (page 203). As a result of 2007 legislative changes (S.L. 2007-213, sec. 6), the second element of this offense should read:

(2) tampers with, removes, vandalizes, or otherwise interferes with the proper functioning of

Related Offenses Not in This Chapter (page 203). Failing to provide information to or cooperate with the Department [G.S. 14-208.44(c)]

CHAPTER 11
CRIME AGAINST NATURE, INCEST, INDECENT EXPOSURE, AND RELATED OFFENSES (PAGE 205)

CRIME AGAINST NATURE (PAGE 207)

Notes (page 207)

Constitutionality (page 207). Application of the crime against nature statute to a minor's consensual sexual activity with another minor does not run afoul of the Due Process Clause of the Fourteenth Amendment to the United States Constitution (361 N.C. 287).

Age and consent (page 208). The offense of crime against nature applies to consensual acts between minors, regardless of the age difference between the minors (361 N.C. 287).

CHAPTER 12
KIDNAPPING AND RELATED OFFENSES (PAGE 223)

FIRST-DEGREE KIDNAPPING (PAGE 225)

Notes (page 226)

Element (1) (page 226). The following should be added to the second paragraph of this note: There was sufficient evidence of confinement when the victim testified that although she asked the defendant to leave her apartment, he continued to stand by the door with his back to the only exit, and the defendant admitted that he closed and locked the apartment door while the victim was inside (___ N.C. App. ___, 646 S.E.2d 123).

The following text should be added to the third paragraph of this note: There was sufficient evidence of restraint when the defendant pinned the victim on a bed by pushing his knee into her chest and grabbed her hair to prevent her from escaping (___ N.C. App. ___, 643 S.E.2d 637).

For another case explaining the difference between confinement and restraint, see ___ N.C. App. ___, 651 S.E.2d 917.

Elements (4)(d) and (e) (page 227). For cases in which the evidence was insufficient to establish that the confinement, restraint, or removal was to facilitate a felony, see ___ N.C. App. ___, 651 S.E.2d 917 (crime allegedly facilitated was completed when the kidnapping occurred), and ___ N.C. App. ___, 646 S.E.2d 123 (same).

Element (5)(a) (page 228). The defendants did not release the victims when they left them bound on the premises (___ N.C. App.___, 645 S.E.2d 93). The defendant did not release the victims by fleeing; the defendant continued to be constructively present because neither the victims nor law enforcement officers were certain about whether he had actually relinquished the victims and vacated the premises (___N.C. App. ___, 640 S.E.2d 797). The defendant did not release child victims by leaving them in an upstairs room where they had been confined while forcing their mothers downstairs one by one; the defendant did not engage in affirmative action to release the children (___N.C. App. ___, 640 S.E.2d 797). The defendant did not release a victim by handing him off to an accomplice from whom the victim later escaped (___N.C. App. ___, 640 S.E.2d 797).

Element (5)(b) (page 228). The trial court did not err in instructing the jury that serious injury is injury that causes great pain and suffering or mental injury where the mental injury extends for some appreciable time beyond the crime; the court was not required to instruct that serious mental injury also must be beyond that normally experienced by victims of the type of crime charged (___ N.C. App. ___, 653 S.E.2d 249).

Multiple punishment (page 229). A defendant could be convicted of kidnapping, burglary, and armed robbery when the restraint inherent in the burglary and armed robbery was separate from that involved in the kidnapping; as to two of the victims, the robbery was complete when the restraint occurred (___N.C. App. ___, 640 S.E.2d 797). Because the defendants bound the victims, the restraint involved with the kidnapping was separate from and not inherent in the armed robbery (___ N.C. App.___, 645 S.E.2d 93). The defendant's restraint and removal of the victim was more than mere technical asportation inherent in an armed robbery (___ N.C. App. ___, 644 S.E.2d 615). The defendant's act of restraint and removal in preventing the victim's escape from her residence, when the armed robbery had not yet begun, was sufficient evidence to support a kidnapping conviction (___ N.C. ___, 651 S.E.2d 879). The defendant's restraint of the victim went beyond that inherent in attempted second-degree rape when after that crime was completed, he pulled the victim away from a couch and dragged her to the kitchen and toward a door (___ N.C. App. ___, 653 S.E.2d 249). By pinning the victim on the bed, grabbing her hair, and preventing her from leaving the motel room, the defendant engaged in restraint separate and apart from the crime of assault by strangulation (___ N.C. App. ___, 643 S.E.2d 637).

The defendant's kidnapping conviction was vacated because any confinement and restraint was inherent in the defendant's assault on the victim and any removal was inherent in the armed robbery of the victim (181 N.C. App. 295).

When the evidence showed that the defendant confined the victim, the court was not required to consider whether the restraint involved with the kidnapping was inherent in another charged felony (___N.C. App. ___, 646 S.E.2d 123).

CHAPTER 13
LARCENY, POSSESSION OF STOLEN GOODS, EMBEZZLEMENT, AND RELATED OFFENSES (PAGE 239)

MISDEMEANOR LARCENY (PAGE 241)

Notes (page 242)

Multiple offenses (page 243). Two separate acts of larceny occurred supporting two convictions when the defendant stole a shotgun from a truck and then entered and stole another vehicle; the defendant's different purposes for taking the shotgun and vehicle suggested that each taking was motivated by a unique criminal impulse or intent (___ N.C. App. ___, 638 S.E.2d 508).

Related Offenses Not in This Chapter (page 246). Motion picture piracy (G.S. 14-440.1)

FELONIOUS LARCENY (PAGE 246)

Notes (page 247)

Element (6)(b) (page 247). A larceny was from the person when the defendant stole cash from an employee who was replenishing an automatic teller machine; the money was in a grocery cart by the employee's side (___ N.C. App. ___, 650 S.E.2d 650).

POSSESSION OF STOLEN GOODS—MISDEMEANOR (PAGE 251)

Notes (page 251)

Element (2) (page 252). For a case holding that the evidence was sufficient to establish the defendant's knowledge that goods were stolen but insufficient to establish that the defendant knew that a gun was stolen, see 176 N.C. App. 642.

For another case in which the evidence was insufficient on the issue of whether the defendant knew that a gun was stolen, see ___ N.C. App. ___, 641 S.E.2d 850. The evidence was sufficient to establish that the defendant knew that tools had been stolen when the tools were visible in the bed of a pickup being driven by the defendant, both the tools and the truck were reported stolen hours before the defendant was stopped in the truck, and the defendant fled after being pulled over (___ N.C. App. ___, 652 S.E.2d 744).

Goods represented by law enforcement as stolen (new note). In 2007 the General Assembly amended G.S. 14-71, effective December 1, 2007, to provide that a person is guilty of a Class H felony if the person knowingly receives or possesses property that was in the custody of a law enforcement agency and that was explicitly represented to the person by an agent of a law enforcement agency as stolen (S.L. 2007-373). As discussed in the note entitled "Attempt" under "Receiving of Stolen Goods—Misdemeanor" on page 255 of the main volume, the most that a defendant previously could be convicted of was attempted receiving or possession.

POSSESSION OF STOLEN GOODS—FELONY (PAGE 253)

Notes (page 253)

Goods represented by law enforcement as stolen (new note). See this note under "Possession of Stolen Goods—Misdemeanor," above, in this supplement.

RECEIVING STOLEN GOODS—MISDEMEANOR (PAGE 254)

Notes (page 255)

Attempt (page 255). Delete this note and add the note entitled "Goods represented by law enforcement as stolen" under "Possession of Stolen Goods—Misdemeanor," above, in this supplement.

RECEIVING STOLEN GOODS—FELONY (PAGE 256)

Notes (page 256)

Attempt (page 256). Delete this note and add the note entitled "Goods represented by law enforcement as stolen" under "Possession of Stolen Goods—Misdemeanor," above, in this supplement.

Supplement to Chapter 13   Larceny, Possession of Stolen Goods, Embezzlement, and Related Offenses

LARCENY FROM A MERCHANT (NEW CRIME)

Effective December 1, 2007, the General Assembly enacted G.S. 14-72.11, creating a new Class H felony of larceny from a merchant (S.L. 2007-373). To save space, the statute is not reproduced here. The elements of the new crime are listed below.

A person guilty of this offense
(1) commits a larceny
(2) against a merchant *and*
  (a) takes property valued at more than $200.00 using a specified exit door;
  (b) removes, destroys, or deactivates a component of an anti-shoplifting or inventory control device to prevent the activation of any such device;
  (c) affixes a product code created to fraudulently obtain goods or merchandise at less than actual sale price; *or*
  (d) the property is infant formula valued at more than $100.00.

The new provision does not define the term "merchant." The exit door referenced in Element (2)(a) is defined as an "exit door erected and maintained to comply with the requirements of 29 C.F.R. § 1910 Subpart E, upon which door has been placed a notice, sign, or poster providing information about the felony offense and punishment provided under this subsection" (G.S. 14-72.11). The term "infant formula" is defined by a cross-reference to 21 U.S.C. § 321(z) (G.S. 14-72.11).

ORGANIZED RETAIL THEFT (NEW CRIME)

Legislation enacted in 2007 added new G.S. 14-86.6 creating two new crimes of organized retail theft (S.L. 2007-373). To save space, the statute is not reproduced here. The new provision became effective December 1, 2007, and applies to offenses committed on of after that date. The new offenses are outlined below.

I. Conspiracy to Commit Retail Theft (new crime)

Elements   A person guilty of this offense
(1) conspires with another person
(2) to commit theft
(3) of retail property
(4) with a value of more than $1,500 aggregated over a 90-day period
(5) from a retail establishment
(6) with the intent to sell the property for gain *and*
(7) takes or causes the property to be placed in the control of a retail property fence or other person
(8) in exchange for consideration.

Punishment   Class H felony [G.S. 14-86.6(a)]

Notes   **Element (1).** See "Conspiracy" in Chapter 5, "General Crimes," of the main volume.

Elements (2) and (3). "Theft" is defined as: "[t]o take possession of, carry away, transfer, or cause to be carried away the retail property of another with the intent to steal the retail property" [G.S. 14-86.5(3)]. "Retail property" is defined as "any new article, product, commodity, item, or component intended to be sold in retail commerce" [G.S. 14-86.5(1)].

Element (4). The value of an item is defined as the "retail value of an item as advertised by the affected retail establishment, to include all applicable taxes" [G.S. 14-86.5(4)].

Element (7). A "retail property fence" is a person or business that buys retail property knowing or believing that retail property is stolen [G.S. 14-86.5(2)].

Forfeiture. Any interest a person has acquired or maintained in violation of the provision is subject to forfeiture under G.S. 18B-504 [G.S. 14-86.6(b)].

Related Offenses Not in This Chapter None

II. Receiving or Possessing Retail Theft Property (new crime)

Elements A person guilty of this offense
(1) receives or possesses
(2) retail property
(3) that has been taken or stolen in connection with a conspiracy to commit retail theft
(4) knowing or having reasonable grounds to believe the property is stolen.

Punishment Class H felony [G.S. 14-86.6(a)]

Notes **Generally.** The notes on "I. Conspiracy to Commit Retail Theft" apply here as well.

Related Offenses Not in This Chapter None

FINANCIAL TRANSACTION CARD THEFT (PAGE 263)

I. Taking or Withholding a Card (page 263)

Notes **(page 264)**

Element (1) (page 264). The evidence was sufficient when it showed that the defendant obtained cards without consent but not that the defendant stole the cards (___ N.C. App. ___, 643 S.E.2d 39).

EMBEZZLEMENT BY PUBLIC OFFICERS AND TRUSTEES (PAGE 273)

Notes (page 274)

Lesser-included offenses (new note). Violations of G.S. 159-8(a) and G.S. 159-181(a) are not lesser-included offenses of this crime (___ N.C. App. ___, 646 S.E.2d 376).

MOTOR VEHICLE CHOP SHOPS (NEW CRIME)

In 2007 the General Assembly enacted G.S. 14-72.7 creating new Class H felonies that apply to, among other things, receiving, possessing, and distributing stolen or altered motor vehicles and motor vehicle parts (S.L. 2007-178). To save space, the statute is not reproduced here. The new law became effective December 1, 2007, and applies to offenses committed on or after that date.

CHAPTER 14
ROBBERY, EXTORTION, AND BLACKMAIL (PAGE 279)

COMMON LAW ROBBERY (PAGE 281)

Notes (page 281)

Element (1) (page 281). A taking occurred when the defendant approached the victim as she was unlocking her car, pressed a handgun into her stomach, grabbed her purse from the passenger seat, and then threw the purse back on the seat when the victim said it contained very little money (___ N.C. App. ___, 641 S.E.2d 376).

Element (3). The state need not prove both violence and intimidation; either is sufficient (___ N.C. App. ___, 650 S.E.2d 650).

The snatching of a necklace worn around a person's neck involves sufficient actual force to constitute robbery; the necklace was fastened around the victim's neck and broke as the defendant ripped it off (___ N.C. App. ___, 650 S.E.2d 845).

When a battery did not induce the victim to part with the property, no common law robbery occurred (___ N.C. App. ___, 650 S.E.2d 650).

ARMED ROBBERY (PAGE 283)

Notes (page 283)

Element (3) (page 283). For a case in which a motor vehicle was found to be a dangerous weapon, see ___ N.C. App. ___, 641 S.E.2d 380.

Timing of elements (page 285). A continuous transaction occurred supporting the conviction when (1) the defendant took a store item but did not brandish a weapon until confronted by a store employee (___ N.C. App. ___, 637 S.E.2d 919); and (2) the defendant and an accomplice took store merchandise without paying for it and were pursued by a store employee into the parking lot, where the defendant shoved the employee to the ground and the accomplice attempted to run over her with a vehicle (___ N.C. App. ___, 641 S.E.2d 380).

Lesser-included offenses (page 285). For another case supporting the statement in this note that assault with a deadly weapon is a lesser-included offense of armed robbery, see 361 N.C. 207.

CHAPTER 15
BURGLARY, BREAKING OR ENTERING, AND RELATED OFFENSES (PAGE 291)

FIRST-DEGREE BURGLARY (PAGE 293)

Notes **(page 294)**

Element (1) (page 294). A constructive breaking and entering occurred when the defendant grabbed the victim and pulled him out of his house (___ N.C. App. ___, 652 S.E.2d 336).

Element (2) (page 294). A constructive breaking and entering occurred when the defendant grabbed the victim and pulled him out of his house (___ N.C. App. ___, 652 S.E.2d 336).

Element (3) (page 294). The following should be added at the end of this note: See also ___ N.C. App. ___, 638 S.E.2d 591.

Element (7) (page 296). For a case in which the court of appeals took judicial notice of the time of sunset and of the end of civil twilight, see ___ N.C. App. ___, 651 S.E.2d 917.

Element (8) (page 298). If the indictment alleges that the defendant intended to commit a specific felony inside, then the State must prove that the defendant intended to commit that felony (___ N.C. App. ___, 652 S.E.2d 336). The evidence was sufficient to establish an intent to commit felonious assault as alleged in the indictment even though it also supported an intent to commit the unalleged crime of murder (___ N.C. App. ___, 651 S.E.2d 917). The evidence was insufficient to show an intent to commit armed robbery *inside* of a home when the defendant pulled the victim outside of the house, thus showing an intent to commit the crime *outside* of the home (___ N.C. App. ___, 652 S.E.2d 336).

CHAPTER 16
FRAUD, FORGERY, FALSE PRETENSES, AND RELATED OFFENSES (PAGE 313)

OBTAINING PROPERTY BY FALSE PRETENSES (PAGE 320)

Notes (page 321)

Element (1) (page 321). The note states that the representation need not be oral or written and may be communicated by action. A false representation was communicated by action when a defendant used a credit card belonging to another person to obtain merchandise from a store; the false representation was that the defendant was authorized to use the card (___ N.C. App. ___, 638 S.E.2d 591).

An additional case supporting the statement that presentation of a worthless check constitutes a false statement is ___ N.C. App. ___, 641 S.E.2d 705.

Actual loss and absence of compensation not required (page 322). An additional case indicating that an actual pecuniary loss by the victim is not necessary for conviction is (___ N.C. App. ___, 641 S.E.2d 705).

RESIDENTIAL MORTGAGE FRAUD (NEW CRIME)

Effective December 1, 2007, the General Assembly enacted the Residential Mortgage Fraud Act, as described below (S.L. 2007-163). To save space, the act, which encompasses G.S. 14-118.10 through 14-118.17, is not reproduced here.

Elements   A person guilty of this offense
   (1) with intent to defraud *and*
   (2) for financial gain
   (3) (a) (i) knowingly makes or attempts to make any material misstatement, misrepresentation, or omission
       (ii) within the mortgage lending process
       (iii) with the intent that any person or entity involved in the mortgage lending process relies on it; *or*

(b) (i) knowingly uses or facilitates or attempts to use or facilitate the use of any misstatement, misrepresentation, or omission
    (ii) within the mortgage lending process
    (iii) with the intent that any other person or entity involved in the mortgage lending process relies on it; *or*
(c) (i) receives or attempts to receive proceeds or funds
    (ii) in connection with a residential mortgage closing
    (iii) that the person knew, or should have known, resulted from the conduct described in (3)(a) or (3)(b).

Punishment A violation involving a single mortgage loan is a Class H felony [G.S. 14-118.15(a)]. A violation involving a pattern of residential mortgage fraud is a Class E felony [G.S. 14-118.15(b)]. A pattern of residential mortgage fraud is one that involves five or more mortgage loans, that have the same or similar intents, results, accomplices, victims, or methods of commission or are otherwise interrelated [G.S. 14-118.11(a)(3)]. The statute provides for forfeiture and for restitution (G.S. 14-118.16).

Notes **Element (1).** The State need not show that any person or entity was harmed financially or that any person or entity relied on the misstatement, misrepresentation, or omission [G.S. 14-118.12(b)].

Element (3) generally. G.S. 14-118.11 defines the relevant terms.

Element (3)(b)(i). Unlike Element (3)(a)(i), for this element the misstatement, misrepresentation, or omission apparently need not be material.

Conspiracy or solicitation. Conspiracy or solicitation to do one of the prohibited acts is punished the same as the completed crime [G.S. 14-118.12(a)(4)]. See "Conspiracy" and "Solicitation of Another to Commit a Felony" in Chapter 5, "General Crimes," of the main volume.

Venue. G.S. 14-118.13 provides for venue for criminal proceedings pursuant to the Residential Mortgage Fraud Act.

Authority to investigate and prosecute. G.S. 14-118.14 provides that on its own investigation or on referral by the Office of the Commissioner of Banks, the North Carolina Real Estate Commission, the Attorney General, the North Carolina Appraisal Board, or other parties, a district attorney may institute criminal proceedings for a violation.

Liability for reporting suspected mortgage fraud. G.S. 14-118.17 provides that in the absence of fraud, bad faith, or malice, a person is not subject to civil liability for filing reports or furnishing other information to a regulatory or law enforcement agency regarding suspected residential mortgage fraud.

Related Offenses Not in This Chapter None

FOOD STAMP FRAUD (PAGE 353)

Legislation enacted in 2007 (S.L. 2007-97) amended the statutes dealing with food stamp fraud (G.S. 108A-53 and G.S. 108A-53.1) to replace the phrase "food stamps or authorization cards" with "electronic food and nutrition benefits."

FRAUDULENTLY OBTAINING TELEPHONE RECORDS (NEW CRIME)

Effective December 1, 2007, the General Assembly enacted the Telephone Records Privacy Protection Act, codified at G.S. 14-113.30 through 14-113.33 (S.L. 2007-374). That act creates new Class H felony offenses pertaining to fraudulently obtaining telephone records and selling fraudulently obtained records. To save space, the statutes are not reproduced here.

FALSE STATEMENT TO PROCURE INSURANCE BENEFITS (PAGE 357)

Related Offenses Not in This Chapter (page 359). Motor vehicle insurance rate fraud (G.S. 58-2-164)

CHAPTER 20
BOMBING, TERRORISM, AND RELATED OFFENSES (PAGE 433)

MAKING A FALSE BOMB REPORT (PAGE 438)

I. Making a False Bomb Report as to a Public Building (page 438)

Notes (page 439)

Relationship between the two versions of this offense (new note). A student who typed a message "Bomb at Lunch" on a school calculator while at school could have been charged under either G.S. 14-69.1(a) or (c); although the defendant could have been charged with making a false report about a bomb in a public building under G.S. 14-69.1(c), the conviction under G.S. 14-69.1(a) was proper because the school was a building covered by G.S. 14-69.1(a) (___ N.C. App. ___, 649 S.E.2d 913).

Element (4) (page 439). "Public building" is defined in G.S. 14-69.1(c).

II. Making a False Bomb Report as to a Nonpublic Building or a Vehicle, Aircraft, Vessel, or Boat (page 439)

Notes (page 440)

Relationship between the two versions of this offense (new note). See this note under "I. Making a False Bomb Report as to a Public Building," above, in this supplement.

MAKING A FALSE REPORT CONCERNING MASS VIOLENCE ON EDUCATIONAL PROPERTY (NEW CRIME)

Effective December 1, 2007, the General Assembly made it a felony to make a false report concerning mass violence on educational property, as described below (S.L. 2007-196). To save space, the statute (G.S. 14-277.5) is not reproduced here.

Elements A person guilty of this offense
  (1) makes a report
  (2) to any person or groups of persons
  (3) that an act of mass violence
  (4) is going to occur
  (5) on educational property or at a school-sponsored activity
  (6) knowing or having reason to know that the report is false.

Punishment Class H felony [G.S. 14-277.5(b)]. The court may order restitution, including costs and consequential damages resulting from the disruption of the normal activity that would have otherwise occurred on the premises but for the false report [G.S. 14-277.5(c)].

Notes **Element (1).** The report may be made by any means of communication [G.S. 14-277.5(b)].

Element (3). The term "mass violence" is defined in G.S. 14-277.5(a).

Element (5). The school-sponsored activity may be a curricular or extracurricular activity [G.S. 14-277.5(b)]. The terms "educational property" and "school" are defined in G.S. 14-269.2 [G.S. 14-277.5(a)(1) and (3)].

Related Offenses Not in This Chapter None

CHAPTER 21
PERJURY, BRIBERY, AND OTHER CRIMES AGAINST THE ADMINISTRATION OF JUSTICE (PAGE 449)

COMMON LAW OBSTRUCTION OF JUSTICE (PAGE 451)

Related Offenses Not in This Chapter **(page 452).** Unauthorized practice of law (G.S. 84-4)

INTIMIDATING WITNESSES (PAGE 452)

Notes (page 453)

Element (1) (page 453). The words "menace" and "coerce" are synonymous with the word "threat" (___ N.C. App. ___, 650 S.E.2d 607). The defendant left a voice mail message for the victim calling her a "stinking nasty bitch" and stating that "you've got me under a $5,000 bond. As soon as I make it, I'm going to give you a God damn taste of your own fucking medicine." The message, combined with evidence of the volatile and violent relationship between the two, was sufficient evidence to support one count of intimidating a witness (___ N.C. App. ___, 643 S.E.2d 637). However, the victim's testimony that the defendant told her "at least ten" times not to testify was not sufficient to show that the defendant threatened her at any other time and thus all of the other counts should have been dismissed (___ N.C. App. ___, 643 S.E.2d 637). For a case in which there was insufficient evidence of alleged "menaces and coercive statements" as alleged in the indictment, see ___ N.C. App. ___, 650 S.E.2d 607.

PERJURY (PAGE 455)

Notes (page 455)

Element (1) (page 455). For a case in which there was sufficient evidence of this element even though the defendant claimed that he did not intentionally misstate the facts regarding his ownership interest in real estate on an affidavit of indigency, see ___ N.C. ___, 652 S.E.2d 212.

False statement on an affidavit of indigency (new note). See ___ N.C. ___, 652 S.E.2d 212 for a case in which a perjury conviction was upheld based on a false statement in an affidavit of indigency. Note that G.S. 7A-456 also criminalizes making a false statement on an affidavit of indigency. For a case in which the evidence was insufficient to sustain a conviction under that statute, see ___ N.C. ___, 652 S.E.2d 212.

RESISTING, DELAYING, OR OBSTRUCTING AN OFFICER (PAGE 460)

Notes (page 460)

Element (4) (page 461). Although this offense covers resisting an arrest, it also includes any resistance, delay, or obstruction of an officer in the discharge of his or her duties (___ N.C. App. ___, 651 S.E.2d 584).

Relationship with assault on a governmental officer or employee (page 461). There was no double jeopardy bar to trying the defendant in superior court for resisting, delaying, or obstructing an officer following her appeal from a district court trial in which she was convicted of that crime and acquitted of assault on a governmental officer; although both offenses were based on the same incident, different evidence supported the two charges (___ N.C. App. ___, 651 S.E.2d 584).

Related Offenses Not in This Chapter (page 462). Injuring or killing a law enforcement agency or assistance animal (G.S. 14-163.1)

FALSE REPORT TO LAW ENFORCEMENT AGENCIES OR OFFICERS (PAGE 462)

Related Offenses Not in This Chapter (page 463). Misuse of 911 system (G.S. 14-114.4)

INTERFERING WITH AN EMERGENCY COMMUNICATION (PAGE 463)

Related Offenses Not In This Chapter (page 463). Misuse of 911 system (G.S. 14-114.4)

CHAPTER 22
WEAPONS OFFENSES (PAGE 471)

POSSESSION OF A FIREARM BY A FELON (PAGE 473)

Notes (page 474)

Element (2) (page 474). There was sufficient evidence to establish possession when, on a cool day, a warm, dry, chrome-plated handgun was found in wet grass six inches from the defendant's hand after he was tackled by officers and the defendant was reaching for the gun (181 N.C. App. 302).

Constitutionality (page 475). The North Carolina Court of Appeals has upheld the 2004 version of the statute in the face of challenges that it was not rationally related to a legitimate state interest, was a prohibited bill of attainder, and violated the Ex Post Facto Clause, due process, equal protection, and the Second Amendment (___ N.C. App. ___, 649 S.E.2d 402). The statute does not violate the Double Jeopardy Clause (___ N.C. App. ___, 647 S.E.2d 679).

POSSESSION OF WEAPONS ON SCHOOL GROUNDS (PAGE 483)

Statute (page 483). In 2007 the General Assembly amended subsection (g) of G.S. 14-269.2, pertaining to exceptions to the weapons ban (S.L. 2007-427 and S.L. 2007-511). The exception in subsection (g)(2) now pertains to firefighters, emergency service personnel, and North Carolina Forest Service personnel and any private police employed by a school (under the previous version, an "educational institution") when acting in the discharge of their official duties. Additionally, 2007 legislation (S.L. 2007-427 and S.L. 2007-511) added exceptions for an individual registered under G.S. Chapter 74C as (1) an armed armored car service guard or an armed courier service guard when acting in the discharge of the guard's duties and with the permission of the college or university, and (2) an armed security guard while on the premises of a hospital or health care facility located on educational property when acting in the discharge of the guard's duties with the permission of the college or university [G.S. 14-269.2(g)(5) and (6)].

| I. Possession of Firearms (page 485) |

Notes (page 485)

Exemptions (page 485). See the discussion immediately above regarding the 2007 legislative changes.

CHAPTER 24
OBSCENITY AND RELATED OFFENSES (PAGE 505)

DISSEMINATING OBSCENITY (PAGE 507)

Notes (page 508)

Element (3) (page 508). A witness's testimony about material alleged to be obscene was sufficient to sustain a conviction under G.S. 14-190.1 without introduction of the exact material alleged to be obscene (___ N.C. App. ___, 647 S.E.2d 440).

THIRD-DEGREE SEXUAL EXPLOITATION OF A MINOR (PAGE 523)

Notes (page 524)

Element (1) (new note). There is no requirement of knowing possession (___ N.C. App. ___, 651 S.E.2d 900). For a case in which there was sufficient evidence that the defendant was in possession of computer images in violation of the statute, see ___ N.C. App. ___, 651 S.E.2d 900).

CHAPTER 25
GAMBLING, BINGO, AND RAFFLES (PAGE 529)

GAMBLING (PAGE 536)

Notes (page 536)

Element (2) (page 536). Poker is a game of chance, not a game of skill (___ N.C. App. ___, 643 S.E.2d 626).

CHAPTER 27
DRUG OFFENSES (PAGE 559)

SALE OR DELIVERY OF A CONTROLLED SUBSTANCE (PAGE 561)

Notes (page 575)

Multiple convictions (page 577). This note states that a defendant may not be separately convicted of both the sale and delivery of a controlled substance arising from a single transaction. Another case supporting this point is ___ N.C. App. ___, 652 S.E.2d 276.

MANUFACTURE OF A CONTROLLED SUBSTANCE (PAGE 578)

Notes (page 578)

Element (2) (page 578). There was sufficient evidence of manufacturing by repackaging when the defendant was seen bagging marijuana and a plastic bag containing marijuana found in his pants pocket was similar to plastic bags found in the apartment (___ N.C. App. ___, 641 S.E.2d 850).

POSSESSION OF A CONTROLLED SUBSTANCE (PAGE 579)

Notes (page 580)

Element (2) (page 580). Additional cases in which there was sufficient evidence of constructive possession include:

- There was sufficient evidence of possession as to both the driver and the passenger of a vehicle in which drugs were found; the State also established constructive possession of controlled substances recovered in a room over which the defendant did not have exclusive control (___ N.C. App. ___, 648 S.E.2d 865).

- The defendant had constructive possession of methamphetamine and precursor chemicals found in a shed owned by someone other than the defendant; the owner found the defendant alone in the shed with the door locked from the inside and after the defendant left the shed, investigators found a jar of unknown liquid on a heater that was warm to the touch and a letter addressed to the defendant containing confidential tax information (___ N.C. App. ___, 649 S.E.2d 1).
- Sufficient evidence showed constructive possession in a trafficking by possession case in which the defendant had nonexclusive possession of the home where the drugs were found (___ N.C. App. ___, 645 S.E.2d 159).
- The evidence was sufficient to establish constructive possession where items were found in a house occupied by the defendant and another man and used by a third person a couple of nights a week (176 N.C. App. 642).

POSSESSION OF A CONTROLLED SUBSTANCE WITH INTENT TO MANUFACTURE, SELL, OR DELIVER (PAGE 585)

Notes (page 585)

Element (4) (page 585). The evidence was insufficient to show an intent to sell or distribute when it revealed that the juvenile was found with a single rock of crack cocaine wrapped in cellophane and $271 in cash (___ N.C. App. ___, 647 S.E.2d 129).

MANUFACTURE, SALE, DELIVERY, OR POSSESSION OF A CONTROLLED SUBSTANCE WITH INTENT TO MANUFACTURE, SELL, OR DELIVER AT OR NEAR A SCHOOL, CHILD CARE CENTER, OR PUBLIC PARK (REVISED TITLE) (PAGE 598)

Legislation enacted in 2007 and effective December 1, 2007, increased the "safe zone" around schools, child care centers and parks from 300 to 1,000 feet (S.L. 2007-375). Additionally, while the offense had applied to a "playground in a public park", the amended version applies to "a public park" and the detailed statutory definition for "playground" has been deleted. Thus the note to Element (5)(c) should be deleted and elements for this offense should now read as follows:

A person guilty of this offense
   (1) is 21 years old or older *and*
   (2) knowingly
   (3) (a) manufactures *or*
      (b) sells *or*
      (c) delivers *or*
      (d) possesses with intent to sell or deliver or manufacture
   (4) a controlled substance

(5) on property used for or within 1,000 feet of the boundary of real property used for
    (a) an elementary or secondary school *or*
    (b) a child care center *or*
    (c) a public park.

TRAFFICKING (PAGE 597)

I. Trafficking in Marijuana (page 600)

Notes (page 600)

Element (2) (page 601). For an additional case in which there was sufficient evidence of transportation, see ___ N.C. App. ___, 643 S.E.2d 49 (rejecting the defendant's argument that there was no evidence showing that he personally transported the marijuana when someone else drove the car, which the defendant did not own; the defendant supplied the marijuana that was in the car and did not contest the fact that he had possession of the marijuana at the time).

Element (5) (page 601). The State established an adequate foundation that a scale used to weigh the marijuana was properly functioning when evidence showed that ordinary scales, common procedures, and reasonable steps to ensure accuracy were used (___ N.C. App. ___, 646 S.E.2d 573).

Once the State introduces evidence as to the weight of the marijuana, the defendant must make an affirmative showing that the weight improperly included excludable material, such as mature stalks [see the note on Element (3) in the book]; if the defendant makes this showing, the issue of weight then becomes a factual question for the jury (___ N.C. App. ___, 646 S.E.2d 573).

MAINTAINING A STORE, DWELLING, VEHICLE, BOAT, OR OTHER PLACE FOR USE, STORAGE, OR SALE OF CONTROLLED SUBSTANCES (PAGE 614)

Notes (page 614)

Element (2) (page 614). In order to determine whether a person keeps or maintains a place the following factors may be considered, none of which are dispositive: ownership and occupancy of the property, repairs to the property, and payment of utilities, repairs, or rent (___ N.C. App. ___, 646 S.E.2d 846). Additionally, the term "keeping" suggests possession that occurs over a period of time (___ N.C. App. ___, 646 S.E.2d 846).

For a case in which the evidence showed only that the defendant occupied the property from time to time and did not establish that he kept or maintained the residence, see ___ N.C. App. ___, 646 S.E.2d 846. In that case, the evidence showed that the defendant was the sole occupant of the residence when the search was conducted, three photographs found in a bedroom showed the defendant in various places in the house, and the defendant's identification and other papers were found there, but none listed the residence as his home address; the State presented no evidence showing that the defendant owned the property or took any other responsibility for it, and in fact a utility bill was found in the name of the defendant's brother. In another case, the evidence was insufficient to establish that the defendant maintained a hotel room that he used with his wife; although the defendant occupied the room one night and was present during the search, there was no evidence that he paid for the room or was a registered guest; it would be speculation to say that the defendant, as opposed to his wife, maintained the room (___ N.C. App. ___, 653 S.E.2d 187).

INHALING TOXIC FUMES (PAGE 621)

Legislation enacted in 2007 and effective December 1, 2007, amended the statute, G.S. 90-113.10, to add ethyl alcohol to the list of covered substances (S.L. 2007-134). Additionally, that legislation modified the statutory exception for use pursuant to the direction of a physician or dentist so that it covers use pursuant to the direction of a "licensed medical provider authorized by law to prescribe the inhalant or chemical substance possessed" (S.L. 2007-134).

POSSESSION OF A TOXIC SUBSTANCE (PAGE 622)

Legislation enacted in 2007 and effective December 1, 2007, amended the statute, G.S. 90-113.11, to add ethyl alcohol to the list of covered substances (S.L. 2007-134).

SALE, ETC., OF A TOXIC SUBSTANCE (PAGE 623)

Legislation enacted in 2007 and effective December 1, 2007, amended the statute, G.S. 90-113.11, to add ethyl alcohol to the list of covered substances (S.L. 2007-134).

MANUFACTURE, ETC., OF AN ALCOHOL VAPORIZING DEVICE (NEW CRIME)

Legislation enacted in 2007 and effective December 1, 2007, enacted G.S. 90-113.10A making it a Class 1 misdemeanor for a person to knowingly manufacture, sell, give, deliver, possess, or use an alcohol vaporizing device [S.L. 2007-134; G.S. 90-113.13 (punishment provision)]. An "alcohol vaporizing device" is "a device, machine, apparatus, or appliance that is designed or marketed for . . . mixing ethyl alcohol with pure or diluted oxygen, or another gas, to produce an alcoholic vapor that an individual can inhale or snort," with specified exceptions (G.S. 90-113.10A). This new offense is not a lesser-included offense of possession of drug paraphernalia (G.S. 90-113.10A).

CHAPTER 28
MOTOR VEHICLE OFFENSES
(PAGE 625)

DRIVING WHILE LICENSE REVOKED OR DISQUALIFIED (PAGE 627)

I. Driving While License Revoked (page 629)

Notes (page 629)

Element (4) (page 630). In a case in which the 2006 amendments to G.S. 20-48 did not apply, adequate proof of notice was made when the State introduced a signed certificate of a Division of Motor Vehicles employee; the certificate stated that the employee deposited notice of the suspension in the mail in a postage-paid envelope addressed to the defendant's address on record with the division (___ N.C. App. ___, 645 S.E.2d 793).

IMPAIRED DRIVING AND RELATED OFFENSES (PAGE 634)

I. Impaired Driving (page 634)

Punishment (page 634). Legislation enacted in 2007 added a new subsection (h1) to G.S. 20-179. Effective December 1, 2007, the new subsection provides that for Level One and Two punishments, a judge may impose, as a probation condition, that the defendant abstain from alcohol consumption for a minimum of 30 days to a maximum of 60 days, as verified by a continuous alcohol monitoring system (S.L. 2007-165).

Notes (page 635)

Element (3) (page 635). Legislation enacted in 2007 amended the definition of "public vehicular area" in G.S. 20-4.01(32) (S.L. 2007-455). The amendment, which is effective December 1, 2007, pertains to the third category of areas discussed in the note. Thus the second to last sentence of the first paragraph of this note should be deleted and replaced with the following: The third category of included property is a road used by vehicular traffic within or leading to a gated or nongated subdivision or community, whether or not the subdivision or community roads have been offered for dedication to the public [G.S. 20-4.01(32)(c)].

V. Habitual Impaired Driving (page 643)

Notes **(page 643) Constitutionality (new note).** The habitual impaired driving statute does not violate double jeopardy, even when prior convictions used to support one habitual impaired driving conviction later are used to support a second such conviction (146 N.C. App. 381; ___ N.C. App. ___, 652 S.E.2d 341). *Blakely v. Washington* does not change this holding (___ N.C. App. ___, 640 S.E.2d 432).

VI. Driving by a Person under 21 Years of Age after Consuming Alcohol or Drugs (page 644)

Punishment **(page 645).** The conflict as to punishment discussed in this note was resolved by 2007 legislation, and it is now clear that the punishment for this offense is as provided in G.S. 20-138.3 (S.L. 2007-493, sec. 20).

Related Offenses Not in This Chapter **(page 646).** Delete the first offense listed and replace it with the following:
Selling alcohol to underage person [G.S. 18B-302(a)]
Giving alcohol to underage person [G.S. 18B-302(a1)]
Purchase, possession, or consumption of alcohol by underage person [G.S. 18B-302(b)]

SERIOUS INJURY BY A VEHICLE (PAGE 646)

I. Felony Serious Injury by a Vehicle (page 647)

Notes **(page 647)**

License revocation (page 647). Delete the text of this note and replace it with the following: Legislation enacted in 2007 amended G.S. 20-19(d) and (e) to require a four-year license revocation upon a conviction of felony serious injury by a vehicle and a permanent revocation upon a conviction of aggravated felony serious injury by a vehicle (S.L. 2007-493).

SCHOOL BUS OFFENSES (PAGE 666)

III. Felony Passing or Failure to Stop for a School Bus (page 668)

Legislation enacted in 2007 (S.L. 2007-382) modified this offense, effective December 1, 2007, to delete the element requiring serious bodily injury. Thus the elements of this offense now are as follows:

(1) willfully
(2) violates G.S. 20-217(a) by
   (a) passing or attempting to pass a stopped school bus *or*
   (b) failing to stop or remain stopped for a school bus *and*
(3) strikes any person.

Supplement to Chapter 28 Motor Vehicle Offenses

IV. Use of a Cell Phone When Driving a School Bus (new crime)

Legislation enacted in 2007 (S.L. 2007-261) added new G.S. 20-137.4 making it a crime to use a cell phone while operating a school bus, as described below. The law became effective December 1, 2007. To save space, the statute is not reproduced here.

Elements

A person guilty of this offense
(1) operates
(2) a school bus
(3) on a public street, highway, or public vehicular area *and*
(4) uses a mobile telephone
(5) while the school bus is in motion.

Punishment

Class 2 misdemeanor, punishable by a fine of not less than $100 [G.S. 20-137.4(f)].

Notes

Element (1). See the note on Element (1) under "I. Driving While License Revoked" in the main volume.

Element (2). The term "school bus" is defined in G.S. 20-4.01(27)(d4) except that it also includes any school activity bus defined in G.S. 20-4.01(27)(d3) and any vehicle transporting public, private, or parochial school students for compensation [G.S. 20-137.4(a)(4)].

Element (3). See the note on Element (3) under "Impaired Driving" in the main volume.

Element (4). "Mobile telephone" is defined in G.S. 20-137.3(a)(2). The statute also covers use of "any additional technology associated with a mobile phone" [G.S. 20-137.4(b)].

Exceptions. G.S. 20-137.4(d) provides that the offense does not apply to the use of a mobile telephone or additional technology associated with a mobile telephone for the sole purpose of communicating in an emergency situation. "Emergency situation" is defined in G.S. 20-137.4(a)(2).

FAILURE TO STOP, MOVE OVER, OR SLOW DOWN FOR AN EMERGENCY VEHICLE (PAGE 668)

In 2007 the General Assembly amended the portion of G.S. 20-157(f) defining "public service vehicle." The amendment deletes the requirement that the vehicle has been called to the scene by a motorist or a law enforcement officer (S.L. 2007-360).

III. Failure to Move Over or Slow Down for a Stopped Emergency or Public Service Vehicle (page 671)

Notes (page 672)

Element (4)(a) (page 672). The definition of a "public service vehicle" has been amended, as described above.